Unearth

A poetry collection

By: Maya Welch

Cover Art done by
Connor Rutledge

Dedications

To Ari for helping me make my dream
become a reality

To my parents for telling me to dream

And to my beloved brothers for believing
that I could

Bury

To put in the ground
and cover with earth; Hide away

The Peak

I sit on the peak and yell out not knowing
Not knowing if my cries will be heard by
The people below, or if my voice will
Sink into oblivion

Hidden

Self-isolation is sitting alone
Knowing you can socialize
And choosing not to

Not Enough Space

"Why is your room so messy?"
Because it's hard
To unclutter your
Space when
You can't even
Unclutter your own
Mind

I pray to God
Every night that
The next day I don't
Have to wrestle my demon.

I'm still praying

Inevitable

It's not the stress itself I fear
But the inevitability of it
That scares me

Home

Home is
Two story
Four bedroom, three bathroom
Six people, one dog, two geese
Home is
An early morning crow
That wakes everyone up
And the late night dog bark
That only disturbs neighbors
Home is
Hay falling like snow
When you toss a flake,
As it gets everywhere you don't want it
Home is
A barn made of scraps
And old miscellaneous things
That brings it only character

Home is also
One story
Three bedroom, two bathroom,
Five people, two dogs, two cats
Home is
The sun shining through the glass door
As the coffee steam slowly rises
While the dog begs for her food
Home is
The first green lawn
Where you can lay down without the mud
And feel the dew collecting under you
Home is
The small house
In the quaint neighborhood
Far from the barn

Home is
The fifteen minute drive
Between the two
Every friday night
Home is
Blasting music
As we sing in the car,
Driving over the line between dirt and pavement
Home is
The bags in the back
That are tossed around,
Holding what we don't have two of
Home is
Ignoring the fact that
This drive used to not be home
And it never should've been
Yet
We sit there with the music blasting
And try to enjoy it all the same

Wanting

You stand there
And ask
"What do you want?"
What do I want?

I want
One house, not two
Two parents, not four
One life not many

I want
To live in peace
Without the dangers of my mind
Overpowering my abilities

I want
This stress to be ripped
Away from my slowly
Decaying body that it
Thinks it can feast on

I want
To go back to my childhood
Where I could still
Hold on to all these things

So.
When you ask
"What do you want?"
I will respond with
"I dont know"
Because when you ask it
Oh so simply
I will answer it
Oh so simply

Father, Hold Me

Do you wonder when was
The last time
You picked her up?
Can you remember?
I don't know if
You do but
I remember when
I had just passed my test retake
You picked me up and
Spun me around in joy

I felt that kind of joy again today
Soaring high in the sky
The smile and the laughter
Was the same just
Without the tears
I wish you were there

I sometimes wonder if that
Was the last time
Youll ever pick me up

I hope not

Is it that I'm much too old?
No longer young enough to
Be picked up?

I wish you could pick me up once
More because
I'm not totally sure
I can always do it
On my
Own
Some days it feels as if
I am the only one who can
Pick myself up
And I'm getting tired

Reach

Soaring.
 Soaring high
  I could almost
   Touch you. I
    Reached and I
     Almost felt that
      Soft everpresent love
       You always had.
        Then
       I had to swing
      Backwards being pulled
     Away a blast of wind
    Blowing in my eyes
   Knowing that
   I would
  Just swing
  Lower
  And
  Lower
  Not quite
  Reaching

Pest

Most say that you
Are a pest.
Someone to be ignored and
Not minded
And that
When you talk it sounds
Like intense laughter

Yet
When I look at you
I see
More than the
Vibrant eyes
More than the all consuming
Ear shattering creature
That you're supposed to be

I see
Your quiet, watchful gaze
Your inquisitive, demanding sound
I see
The misunderstanding surrounding you

Yet there you stand
Laughing
In the faces of those who
Say that you are a pest

Objects in Mirror are Closer than they Appear

Slowly approaching
Never stopping
Getting closer
Never reaching

Mirror, Mirror

Towel wrapped around my body, the mirror right in front of me. I can see from the middle of my forehead to the bottom of the towel surrounding my thighs. I stare at this girl in the mirror right in her eyes. Whenever I've done this in the past, I immediately looked away because I couldn't bear to look at her. But I stared at her bloodshot eyes and red face. I looked at the way her messy wet hair fell onto her face, the way she didn't brush it away letting the water drip onto her breasts. I looked into her eyes again. I saw the redness from hours of crying. From feeling stressed, from feeling exhausted, from feeling alone. I saw the purple under her eyes from the tears that seemed to flow endlessly, each drop sliding down, making the purple a darker shade.

I could see in her eyes the way she seemed to drag herself through each day, each week, each month. The way she was done with dragging her limp body. But, I also saw determination in her eyes. The way she still held her head up, the way she wasn't done fighting just yet, the way she didn't want to lose whatever she may be fighting. Never have I stared at this girl so long. It used to scare me everytime I did. When I did I only saw something that shouldn't be looked upon, something that was sad and miserable. But now when I look upon her all I see is hope for something better. Just because her eyes are red and teary, doesn't mean she is sad, it just means she is trying. I can see why this girl isn't desirable, but with that I can see why she is.

Time

I've learned that
There is not near enough
Time in this world
To feel depressed

The Hole

In one instant you're there
                The next you're not
You slide   through the fingers of
Life and   you fall
        And   fall
        And   fall
        And   fall
Until SMACK and you're
Not sure what but you
Know there is no getting back
because you are
Now at THE END

Stars 

She lay in her bed, machines whirring, buzzing, beeping their melancholic tune. I caress her cold soft hand, feeling her heartbeat get slower and slower.

"What do you think the afterlife is like grandma?" I ask.

"What do you mean sweet child?"

"I mean after you die, what do you think happens to you?"

"Oh sweet thing, I will not die," I look at her confused, because of course we die, how can we not?

"I will not die," she said again. "When I fall asleep,

I'm going to go up to the stars.

I'm going hop

from star

to

star,

never slowing down to catch a breath.

Each star I step on will glow with a brightness

that overpowers the others.

I will feel every part of my body that hurts and aches start to heal and fix itself. Each star will hold my weight as I balance on it looking down on the world.

And when I do, all the lights down here will look like the
twinkling stars I'll be
dancing on.

 I will feel joy
Such joy that I will 
jump
and spin,
letting the wind blow me in a whirl of color and light
as I swirl with them. I will do this every night
letting it take me,
and I will never grow old or brittle.

I'll stay
young and springy.
I will be the most alive I have ever been.
So you see, I cannot die. Even though I won't be here, I will continue to live."

With that her heart stopped and the long beep came.

And yet I did not see death, in her eyes.

I saw stars dancing endlessly through the night with all the souls of the world.

Accumulate

To gather, forming a steadily
increasing quantity

Understand

Hold me
Caress me
Let me feel your soft touch

Talk to me
Whisper to me
Let me hear your smooth words

Look at me
Stare at me
Let me feel your eyes wander

Soothe me
Warm me
And I promise you won't go under

Listen to me
Understand me
Say that you love me

We Feel It Too

Why is it
That
Teenage love and
Teenage heartbreak
Are always considered
Stupid and not real?

Is it stupid then
To care for someone
When you are young?
Is it stupid then
To cry yourself to sleep
Even though you aren't experienced?

No?
Yet to be in love
And to be heartbroken
While new to it, is stupid?

Tell me then,
If it's so stupid,
Why do I
Feel it so
Violently?

Results

When I asked you
"What does love feel like?"
I might as well of
Asked you
"What does heartbreak feel like?"

Numb

I need to remember how to feel again

H.A.P.P.Y.

Horrible
Acting
Purposely
Playing
You

Leaving Me

Hearing you start to mutter
I know you're hiding your color

But oh! I must ignore all you say
Because I need you to stay

How I hope it'll just pass
This feeling that shouldn't last

Wishing for you to hear my song
But oh! Where did I go wrong?

It must've been the deeds
They say that plant evil seeds

I should've known better
After reading the holy letter

And yet despite deaths's sins
I followed my mortal whims

So here I am stuck with you
Not wanting to follow through

But oh! I must be punished
For staying with someone
I never should've trusted

Broken Promises

You promised me you.
You said I was yours,
But now you've left me and
I'm forced to wait here
Hands full of broken promises

You promised there was
No one else you thought of,
Though you never were a cheater,
You still hold her hands
And kiss her lips
Yet, I'm only given broken promises

You promised your support
Something that was endless
Yet I made my own decision
And you could not agree
What was best
Leaving me to pick up broken promises

You promised me your love
And that I'd receive it no matter what
Yet here I am
Navigating your broken promises

Wrong

Every time I looked at you
I knew
I could never be mad
At you

Oh how wrong
I can be

Stage 6: Revenge

You stand before me as if you've
Done nothing corrupt
As if you should mock me
Of my broken soul
You come to ridicule me for my
Melancholic despairs
Oh Lord! Cast away my pains!
Oh! How I wish! To take out
Your heart in front of your eyes
And make you watch it as it pumps
The last of its blood
Watch it wilt as a dying flower
That browns quickly with time
And after that I shall rip
Your soul from your ribs
And there I shall hold it like that of paper
Slowly
Piece
By
Piece
I shall rip it to
Tiny parts

And there before you
I shall cast the rotten flesh
And the torn pieces aside
There shall you drop to your knees
In despair and cry out,
"Oh! How can I be loved again by someone
With a heart and soul like this?"
Maybe then you will know
My pains and sorrows!
You are a man that your word
Is not your covenant!
A man that casts away the souls
That are given to him!
So cast your soul to the devil!
A man such as you deserves
The burning of hell
And not to live a life so well

Objection

I am not a simple object
To parade about and
Show to your friends
If
I was an object I am not
A simple one that lacks
Feelings you don't want to hear
Or
For me to express

I am not an object
I am not something to be
Merely
Stared at and touched
Whenever you so please
I am not something
For you to command
And for me to follow
Your every whim

I am not something
That will stand down when
You call
My leadership
                Bossy
My passion
                Bitchy
My fight
                "Won"

I will not stand here as
You walk all over me
Saying "You have power"
Like you would to a
Simple object

Lucky

It takes a
Lucky man
To see the beautiful
Girl she is
And how charming
She can be

It takes an
Unlucky man
To see
Her wrath

Deserted

It is sad
That I must leave you
Though I have the
Rest of my life to
Accomplish

I will miss
The way you
Kissed my skin so
Warmly and
So tenderly

I will miss
The way you
Held me close
Not letting me drift
Too far off

I will miss
Looking up
At you to see
The many beautiful
Wonders you hold

How I wish to take you
With me but,
Alas
I cannot

Maybe one day
The sands of time will
Move you to me
But for now
You're stuck where you are

So I will say my goodbyes now
And hope that one day
We will meet
Again

Broken Pieces

If you look into my eyes
Long enough
And look past my broken pieces
There you will find my
Veins and arteries as
They all twist and swerve
Carrying the precious blood to
My heart; the muscle constantly pumping.
When you look upon it
Please
Do not let the many
Broken pieces of it
Scare you
And when my sorrows start to
Take over, and the blood in
The heart starts to leak from its cracks
Filing my body with its
Red glistening shimmer
Please
Do not let it disturb you
When my despair reach my
Eyes, where everything will pour out
As streaks of red
Flow down my face
Revealing all of my
Broken pieces

Necessity

I used to want to show
You just how much I
Needed you

Now I want to show
You just how much I
Have grown without you

Leaving You

It took me too
Long to get here,
To feel confident
In myself without
You

But when looking back

I realize

I never was confident
To begin with

So

I have left all
Of the good and bad
You gave me
And
Have decided being
My own person
Is better than
Being the person
I was
With you

Who

If you saw me now
You would not recognize me

You would not see the
Girl who
Cried on your shoulder
And shook in your arms

You would not see the
Girl who
Got so overwhelmed
She could not speak

You would not see the
Girl who
Told you I love you
A million times over

Maybe
When you
Look at me now
You think *bitch*
Or *desperate*

You may think
She is
Too much to
Handle

But I promise you
If you saw me now
You would not recognize me

If

I can't see you
If
You don't look at me

I can't hear you
If
You don't speak to me

I can't listen to you
If
You can't open up

I can't learn from you
If
You can't listen

I can't take you seriously
If
You make all things a joke

I can't support you
If
You can't support others

I can't believe in you
If
You don't believe in me

I can't be kind to you
If
All you do is hurt me

I can't learn to love you
If
I hate you

I can't love you
If
You are all of these things

However you are not
Therefore I love you

Dig

To make one's way by removing material

Before the Womb

If I had wings
I would fly
I would let them spread out
So I could let the wind pick me up
Carry me away to
A place that I've always called home
To a town miles away
To a country unknown
Where I can speak a language
So completely foreign to me
I would float to a place where
When my name is spoken to me
It'll be soft as a falling feather
I will follow the path to where,
Despite the violence and fear,
Dragging me down to earth
And despite the worries and troubles
Snipping at the feathers in my wings
I can continue to soar higher than
My wings would allow me

Mother, Show Me

Show me a path to
A place away from the edge
Of this stormy sea

Show me a way to
Stop the dark clouds
From covering the sun

Show me how to
Calm the waves and
Let the water be still

Show me what to
Do when none of this
Works in my favor

Then, show me a path to
The middle of this sea
So that I can control it

Show me what it means to be free

Human Nature

Why is it that
When we say
 She's a woman, she's a human too!
It means that humans are perfect
And whole
But
When she messes up
We say
 She's only human
It means we are prone
To mistakes?
What does it mean to
Be human then?

Cycle

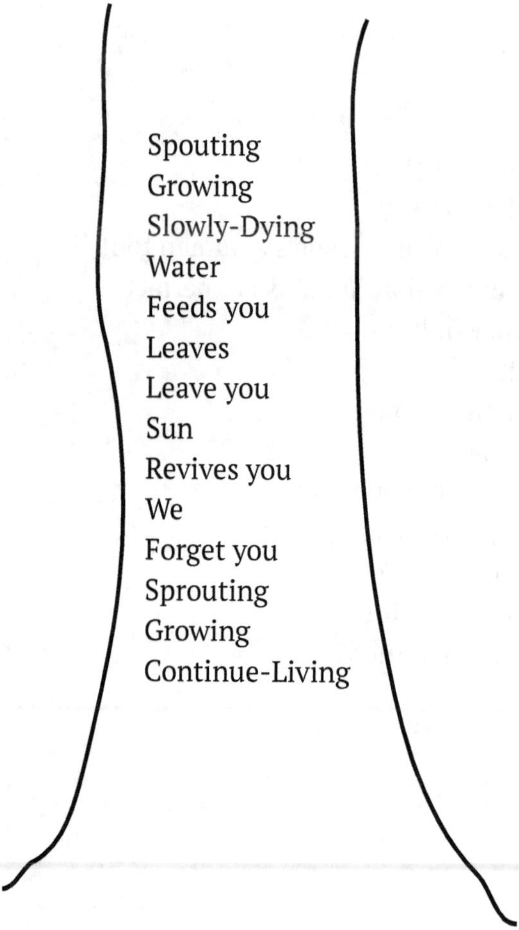

Spouting
Growing
Slowly-Dying
Water
Feeds you
Leaves
Leave you
Sun
Revives you
We
Forget you
Sprouting
Growing
Continue-Living

Womanhood

Follow me to where
My ancestors were laid
And there you
Will find how my history was made.
How it was written in the stars above,
A promise, a weapon
I couldn't overcome.
Oh and the thing that made it so?
The blood that dropped
Like fallen snow
And in the darkness it burned so bright
It was a challenge
I knew I shouldn't fight.
Yet despite its gory red,
The stories I heard and
How I'd wish I were dead,
When the flow hit, without doubt
I was elated and lifted
As I gave out a shout,
"I knew I'd be something to fear!
A mass, a force to be reckoned with,
Somewhere you shouldn't be near!
I told you world I could
Because here and now
I present my womanhood."

A Gift

Curled up into a little ball
Cold eating away at her
She shivers and waits
Waits for the sun to burst forth
To bring her the gift of warmth
Toes curled together
Legs on top of the other
Arms pressed between thighs and chest
Little heat seeps in
But the cold keeps biting

Rain starts to sprinkle
Pattering her face with its droplets
She shivers and waits
Waits for a cover
To bring her the gift of safety
Body out in the open
Vulnerable to everything that hits
Clothes cling tightly to her skin
Now a little less exposed
But the cold keeps biting

Darkness looms ahead
Sun starts to die out
She shivers and waits
Waits for the moon to step forward
To bring her the gift of light
Eyes searching and not seeing
Unable to find a way out of the darkness
Slowly adjusting her senses
Hearing the rain and cool breeze
But the cold keeps biting

Clouds keep still
Refusing to move away
She shivers and waits
Waits for an arm around her
To bring her the gift of love
Blood still runs cold
Believing she'll always be alone
Images of another body pop up
Hoping for a source of warmth to comfort
But the cold keep biting

Shatter

Ripple. Ripple.
You look just like glass
Ripple. Ripple.
You'll break it going so fast

Ripple. Ripple.
I don't think I should touch
Ripple. Ripple.
God I wish I didn't think this much

Ripple. Ripple.
I can see everything you're reflecting
Ripple. Ripple.
Won't you please stop rejecting?

Waves

Water-Stillness.
Swells-Rising.
Waves-Moving.
Breaks-Falling.
Crashing-Drowning.
Bubbles-Rising.
Take me with you.

Show Me a River

Take me down to the river
And show me what
It means to pray
Even though you believe
In no god

Show me the river
As it surges and rushes and
Tell me that I can swim it
As a struggle to keep my head up

Clothe me in your fake
White garments
And tell me that you will baptize
Me in my sorrows and fears
As I slowly drown, air escaping me

Show me all the fresh
Scars you intend to open
And tell me they are not bleeding
As it pours forth from my body

Can't you see it now?
Can't you see it yet?
You fight and scream
Shimmer and gleam
Never waiting on nobody
You see it now
It's very clear
You are the river's daughter

Reflection

I stand at the edge of the water
And look down
To see my reflection staring back.
I have stood at this edge before
And had jumped into the water
I would jump too soon
And fly high,
But as I came down,
I was met with deceiving
Icy
Cold
Water
That froze me as I entered.

So I stand at the edge of the water
Contemplating
Jumping in again even though
It had hurt me several times
Before
But despite the pain
I made out alive so,
How bad can it be?
I take a step back from
The water and
Get a running head start,
And I jump.
I jump higher than I ever had.
Only time will tell if
The water is the same or different this time.

Grow

I need to show
Just how much
I can really grow

Okay

I stand here not knowing

And that's okay

Life

Let go of pain
Ignore sickness
Forget about death
Embrace life

Definition

Maya Grace Welch (n):
~~Someone who has suffered heartbreak, loss, and parent divorce. Prone to anxiety induced seizures and stressing over everything. Depressed; alone.~~

Maya Grace Welch (n):
Love; Grace; Soul; Spirit. Someone who overcomes obstacles, expresses joy, and loves everyone, including herself. Prone to living life to the fullest and having a smile on her face. Loving; graceful.

Unearth

To uncover or bring to light

I stand up here at the top
And look.
Above the storm
Crackles and booms
Clouds

Roiling
Flashing
Lightning streaking down

I scream
And when I cry out
No one hears me
If a tree falls in the forest
Does it make a sound if no one is around?

The rain starts pouring
The drops fall and roll down
My bare and exposed back.
I drop to my knees

The water
Drip. Drip. Drips.
Down my face
Mixing with my tears
Collecting at the bottom of my

Chin and
Dropping to my
Breasts, where the salt seeps
Into my aching heart
The water rolls off

Collecting below my
Mud soaked knees

The thunder roars again
Threatening to throw me down
And tear me apart
I plea as the rain soaks me
And the sounds echo
And the clouds close in

I am trapped at the top
Knees too weak to stand
Eyes too tired to close
Heart too broken to continue
Everything
Swirls
Drops
Rages
And there I am in the
Middle of it all

And when I can't take it anymore
And am about to give up
I stand up one last time
Lift my head up high
And scream out.
My voice echoes:
Love against hate

With rage and fury,
Fire and passion
Every little thing that brought
Me down escapes

Off my tongue and into
The storm
It bounces through the clouds
Off the Earth and
Into the Heavens

The ground trembles beneath me
Yet for once my legs stay strong.
The lightning stops mid strike

The thunder is drowned out
And the clouds stop their
Rampage.

"Look
At the source
Of such a
Hurting
Demanding
Monstrous
Sound
Unlike any other.
Why must it sound like this?" they ask.

"Because you struck fear into my heart.
You decided to
Overcome me
Shame me
Scar me
So I will respond to such atrocities
By screaming my pain to you,
Because assuming I won't fight back
Is an utter mistake," I roar.

And as my scream dies
Out, so does my strength,
And my knees buckle
One last time
And I tumble off the top,
Back to Earth.
My body hits the ground
With a deafening thud.

I lay there on the ground as I
Open my eyes to see the clouds
Far gone-
Their thunder a distant, forgotten sound
I close my eyes again and let my body
Sink back into the earth
Without crying out
Knowing it's where I belong
And that no one heard me fall

Because
If a tree falls in the forest
Does it make a sound if no one is around?